DATE DUE

APR 0 9 1997

TOWN & COUNTRY MATTERS

TOWN

COUNTRY
MATTERS

erotica  satirica

John Hollander

DAVID R. GODINE

The following poems have appeared in periodicals: 'Sonnets to Roseblush,' *Poetry*; 'Sonnets,' *TriQuarterly*; 'Making It,' *Paris Review*; 'New York,' *Harper's*; 'The Loss of Smyrna,' *Intransit*. The translation of Catullus 33 was published in *Movie-Going and Other Poems* (Atheneum, 1962). Permission to reprint is acknowledged.

The drawings on pages 27, 31, and 35 were made by Anne Hollander.

DAVID R. GODINE PUBLISHER
Boston, Massachusetts
Copyright © 1972 by John Hollander
ISBN 0–87923–058–4
LCC 72–82864

CONTENTS

TOWN & COUNTRY MATTERS

NON SUM QUALIS ERAM BONA IN URBE NORDICA ILLA

O for the perfumes that arise
From all those extra-specialty shops
    In Copenhagen!
O for the welcome looks from eyes
Like blue, unbuyable lollipops
    In Copenhagen!
O for those northernmost of fires,
Burning to ashes the binding briars,
Exploding in roses of joys and desires
    In Copenhagen!

O for the peachy, smooth behinds
Awaiting us, all trembling there
    In Copenhagen!
O for the melons minus rinds
And tummies plumper than the pear
    In Copenhagen!
O for the blood of strawberries,
Dripping across the palest knees,
Bent for the birch's ecstasies
    In Copenhagen!

O for the raincoats, stiff and black,
Along the glittering, rainy streets
    Of Copenhagen;
O for the bared, Swinburnian back
Entranced beyond the dreams of Keats

By Copenhagen;
O for the bars where Aquavit
Can cool the gaze that flames with heat
When turned on tight, high-buttoned feet
        In Copenhagen!

O for the many wild and arty
Combinations, all allowed
        In Copenhagen;
Ten's company, and twelve's a party,
And only ninety-three's a crowd
        In Copenhagen;
O for the circuses and scenes
Involving visiting marines
And girls with recherché machines
        In Copenhagen!

O for the splendid substitutes
For all the old, familiar tricks
        In Copenhagen;
Do-it-yourself kits that are beauts
For all the merry heretics
        Of Copenhagen;
O for the objects, strange and new,
The pencils that will strip for you
And show some creature's thing or two
        From Copenhagen!

O for that forward-looking land
Where willing nightingales still sing
        In Copenhagen;
O for the firm, directing hand,

The eye that's on the coming thing
   In Copenhagen;
Where there is neither want nor fear
And oddity's a great career—
Lord, may we live to spend next year
   In Copenhagen!

[1960]

MAKING IT
a proem to something longer

Once, but once, did I fail my Muse, who, lying
(Golden-shadowed shape) by the flaring candle,
Urged me upward. But there was more to dying
    Than I could handle.

Girl of gold, you worked such a leaden vengeance
On my poor pen three weeks ago: I tried to
Raise it. No. Despite your presumed attentions
    All I could ride to

Was the jangling creak of a bedspring, failing
Sounds not even mine, that were made to shake it
On some record, behind a swish youth's wailing.
    Help me to make it!

How the candle guttered and died! Its throbbing
Flame had dripped a sadness of wax that crowned us
Both with hot, red drops of its final sobbing:
    Heavens around us

Seemed just then to flicker a stormy warning.
Was it that? Or was it the candle's trembling,
Making instant shiftings from night to morning,
    Never dissembling

Really, but immersed in imaginations?
Fireworks sprouting visions aloft, and breaking

Up the mindless night with illuminations,
    Feigning, not faking,

Never can quite vanish completely for us,
After-images will outlast the hissing
Violence of rocketing lights, the chorus,
    Sighing and kissing.

Come then, let us celebrate all this fire:
Not to do it now would be to deny it.
Mirror, bed and discarded clothes conspire,
    Beg us to try it.

Help me now, dear girl; neither pot nor liquor
Turns the poem on, helps us to get connected.
All our golden cities are growing sicker.
    Am I infected?

Are you down with something? I'm feeling seedy,
As I grope through blankets of silence. Bend, O
Unforgiving prescence! But no: *Perdidi*
    Musam tacendo

(Help me!) *nec me Apollo respicit* (as A-
Nonymous once whispered, a played-out Roman);
I, laid-up New Yorker, feel that it has a
    Touch of the omen,

This half-buried failure of mine to make it,
One July night, tangled up with the legs of
Her who was my Muse once. We both must take it.
    Using the dregs of

Sour wines of embarrassment, and refusing
Drinks from untipped cups of delight, my shaking
Hand must mix some cocktail of your own choosing,
      And of my making;

Drink; then do and die. If I've been too clever
This should make me stop, for my stomach's queasy:
Making something up out of nothing's never
      Happy or easy.

[1962]

NON BONA DICTA...
a few from catullus

16

Go shove it up! Go eat it, both of you,
Fancy Aurelius and Furius the Fruit
Who judge me by my dirty poetry!
For if an honest poet must be straight,
Poetry needs no honor; it should be
Both curious and queer enough, and hot
To tickle greybeards with (and I do not
Mean boys, but men whose legs can hardly twist,
Being so stiff). Because you have read through
A thousand kisses, why do you insist
That I'm a faggot like the pair of you?
Go shove it up! And then go eat it too!

Please love, please, Ipsithilla sweet,
Right at noon call me and we'll meet
At once; and, love, just one thing more—
Make very sure that your front door
Will be unlocked, that you won't think
You've got to dash out for a drink
Or something. Wait there for our feast
Of nine continuous fucks at least.
But ring me quickly; I'll come flying:
Breakfast is over, and I'm lying
Flat on my back now, and it shows,
Sticking out through all my clothes.

33

O best of thieves, Vibennius, Père,
Who haunts the Baths, and you that rare
And ruined son of his, look here!
(Papa's right hand is quick to err
 But Junior's tail is greedier.)
Get out of town! For we know what
It is that Pa keeps snatching at
And that your furry bottom, sonny,
Can't be sold for love or money.

58

Caelius, our old Lesbia, The Lesbia,
Lesbia, the one that Catullus loved
More than himself and all he called his own—
Now, both in alleys and at intersections,
Pulls off all the upright sons of Rome.

59

Rufa goes down on Rufulus (and she
Meninius' wife); often you'll see
How at a funeral she gets supper free.
While she grabs goodies from around the grave
She's clobbered by the undertaker's slave.

80

Why do those rosy lips, O Gellius, grow
More white, each morning, than the winter snow,
Or when, toward evening, finally you abjure
Your comfy daylight nap? I can't be sure—
Is rumor right that you go down upon
The eight great inches of a common man?
Well, yes. The proof? Poor Victor's thing is numb,
Those famous lips are both dried white with come.

88

When with Mama and Sister all night long
One does things with one's clothes off, Gellius,
What goes on? When he's put horns on Uncle,
How rotten, Gellius, can someone get?
Fouller by far than even distant Tethys
Or Oceanus, Father of every water,
Could decontaminate. There's no worse crime,
Not even to bow your head and blow yourself.

89

Worn out is Gellius. And why not? With Mother
So willing, kind and spry, Sister so sweet,
Uncle so generous, with Aunt, and the other
Girls that he knows, how could he not look beat?
Keeping to what should be 'hands off' alone,
He manages to look like skin and bone.

TWO BRIEF TALES

prologue

Last night, inside her Fortune-Teller's booth
Outside the Freakshow, wailing her lost youth,
Circe lamented:
     'What's a girl to do
When, after dinner, all Ulysses' crew
Giggling, turn pigs (as unbecomingly
As my revealing magic made them be
The emblems of their moral lives)? We start
When cruder life begins to mimic art,
But I am done when actuality
Takes on the shapes that satire makes us see—
Young Scylla, bathing her impatient snatch,
No longer shudders as my arts attach
Voracious dogs' heads to her yapping mound,
Her thighs dissolving into packs of hound.
Instead, she plies her own cosmetic skill,
Paints Error's forest over Venus' hill;
Her thighs turn shackles and—the latest stunt—
A gothic hell-mouth yawns around her cunt.
Why picture truth? What's transformation for
When every wife proclaims herself a whore?
When parodies of explanation turn
Out to be plausible, what can we learn
From shoddy magic that I used to use
To turn life inside out with, as the Muse
Of Metamorphosis? Now I sit out
My days here in this tent, the roustabout
And burly circus-driver at my gate,
As *Madame Foofoo, she who will relate*

All past, all future. But inside my dark
Trailer, the emptied, still amusement park
Outside lit only by a bulb or two,
I tell myself a story from the few
Last uncompleted changes—tales that turn
Passions with which even immortals burn
Into the torches in whose light poor mortals learn.'

turning green

for William Styron

Apollo, having seen his Daphne grow
Green leaves above and chaster bark below
(Emblem of poets whose desire can turn
Into strange greenness that for which they burn),
Pined for her sister nymph; but, truth to tell,
He'd learned his vegetable lesson well:
Eschewing any chase direct, lest she
Likewise turn wooden, unembracing tree
Shadily frowning on all amorous scenes,
He chose to be converted into greens.
Nor swinging poplar, nor the dappled mass
Of garden flowers, nor the furry grass
Did the bright god reform himself among,
But in a low vine, humble and unsung.
Stiffness untiring, members without number
(Even Olympian erections slumber)
Grow, earth-embracing, all about the sweet cucumber—
And thus he makes the verdant nymph his own:
Behold her, overcome and overgrown—
In, out, in marbled forms and parts hirsute,
From front and back—with green and longing fruit.

VIRIDIA VIRILIA CONVERSA

a piscatory problem

for Frank Kermode

One day the fisher-swain, young Glaucus, bore
His nets and troubles to the stony shore
To drown his tears and dissipate his sighs
In surfy groans and sea-gulls' heartless cries.
 'O woe!' (said he) 'that she I loved should be
Lost in th'uncaring vastness of that sea!
Poor Phyllis flung herself into the deep
From yonder cliff, with a distracted leap,
And vanished while, below, about that rock
Foam, like the tatters of her lacy frock,
Ebbed back and forth while the advancing spray
Upraised its fragile mantle in dismay;
Since when each day I visit here to mourn
My long dissolved love, my hope forlorn.'
   A quiet tune, not unmixed with the wind
Then 'gan to wander gently toward his mind;
A murmuring maiden in the foam he spied
Whose liquid melody arose and died,
Now grave, and now acute like laughing spray:
Then, with a splash, a dainty mermaid lay
Beside him on the rocks. Her sea-green eyes
Dazzled his own; the watery paradise
Of her dark weedy hair invited him
To leave his sorrows, enter there, and swim.
 'Old Nereus' (she said) 'has given me
As some small compensation from the sea
That reft you of your love, so we may play

Here in these grottoes, where the light of day
Half-enters, as if but to peep inside,
Half-laughing, half-abashed at what he spied
Within its depths, at what things he has seen
Done to the mermaid, heard sounds that have been
Conscious of Nereids flopping on the shores.
Come in. My name is Doris. I am yours.'
    So from the azure ocean, that deep mind
Dreaming of its green counterparts, we find
Resemblances of all our joys departed:
The swain reached out, fair-headed and light-hearted,
To clutch the mermaid to him, but her tail
Engendered yet one more lamenting wail:
 'Leaving the forests of your waving hair,
My hands would voyage through your everywhere;
But having landed on those two white isles
Whose rosy summits fill the air for miles
With beckoning fragrance, I would yet sail on
Southward toward final tropics, ever drawn
Down toward the lovely garden, yet I freeze
Lost in the green chill of these scaly seas
Toward which such promising white meadows sink,
Then lose themselves in the unwanted drink.
There, where two limbs' division should begin
That joys might multiply, united in
Mock-marriage, this one fishy tail divides
Lovers more cruelly than peaks or tides.
The temple of your body has no crypt
Nor holy river, wherein may be dipped
My eager sacrifice, which, rising high
In holy contemplation, seeks to die.'
    Thus baser is the higher part of love,

Imprisoning caresses far above
The pit they seek: erotic paradox,
Wrecking love's pinnace on its hidden rocks!
   But laughed the nymph: 'Such baseless logic stay!
Love finds the higher, not the lower way;
Venus, as wise still as her power is strong,
Raised her true palace in the Place of Song
Where kissing portals and a welcoming tongue
Invite love's visitor to rest among
The coral caverns and the pliant bed
Of Love and Wisdom, wedded in the head.'
Leading still-wondering Glaucus by the hand
Into a rocky cave hard by the strand,
The nymph, as in the emblem, with a kiss,
Led him to port in her sea-bower of bliss.

ET SAPIENTIÆ TEMPLO MANET AMOR

SONNETS FOR ROSEBLUSH

I

Since bed's the only world of pure idea
That history has left us; and our forms,
Glowing invisibly in darkness here,
Alone transcend the black, galactic storms,
The last two universals; to conclude
That you're unreal except when both my hands
Are clapped around your ass and lassitude
In a mad world of shadows shows us lands
That lie below Atlantis, just this side
Of sleep, is no Platonic sloppiness:
Not come to bed yet, after having died,
You're only human, and I'm somewhat less;
Until this sheet, with both of us upon it,
Tosses us essences into a sonnet.

2

Like the bright Ladies of the Sonneteers
Who only became real inside a poem,
You stop existing during all those years
Between the Jubilees when we're at home
In bed, at work, or play (depending on
Love's season). What you do out there by day
Is literary; walking to the john
Or getting up to shut the window's gay
Romantic fiction. Truth and circumstance
Are here and now, upon this mattress, where
(Uncross your legs while I pull down your pants)
Fabric of vision yields to skin and hair.
Nature is what we're doing; it takes art
To dream a life of which this act's a part.

3

I thought of turning you into a boy
So that my queer friends, too, might feel the quick
Of my longing when they read this, and the joy
Of my having. But it's much too hard a trick
Just as it is, to keep you breathing fast,
Moving beneath me on this bed of paper.
My lady is too volatile to last;
How can I risk her substance to reshape her?
Yes, that means you, sweet. I can feel you twist
Against me still and freeze in a brief cry,
My true deep secret that does not exist:
Why should I break you out into a lie?
No. Ed and Fred and Ted and Ike and Mike
Will just have to imagine what it's like.

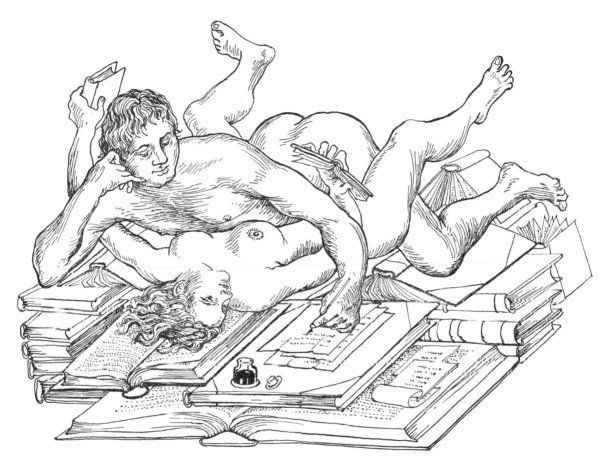

LIBER AMOREM LIBERAT

4

I can do you and Dame Philosophy
At once, without incurring jealousy:
Inside his girl, any poor student finds
That other bodies aren't other minds.
Just so, I've learned that what it is I feel
When fitted into you's the same old real
World that my elbow on the mattress tells me
Can't lie, or change its mind, the world that quells me
When, in contracting, it can seem to know
Me in the sense I know you're here below.
I can be your pain; you are still my world.
Our mixed-up categories lie here, curled
Not in real sympathy, but just in touch:
After too long, it gets to be too much.

5

Were Sade and Sacher-Masoch Jacobins
For nothing? Shoulder to shoulder, on the shelf,
Justine and *The Furred Venus* bare their sins.
One smashed the Other, the other one, the Self,
Yet both were enemies of bondage, when
That bondage was not self-imposed. Below
This row of moralists, now and again
We took our sad and learnèd pleasures, though
The usual feudal screwing might have bored
Sade, whom tight bands of passion bound to his victim
Or Masoch (when he'd made his lady lord)
Whose will wielded the thorns with which she pricked him.
Egalitarian enough for two,
Sometimes, love, I'll insist on what we'll do.

6

Charlus, chained to his bed at Jupien's—
No man, we're told, has ever been more free.
I don't know how this paradox extends:
My magnet hand, sliding above your knee
Toward a far stronger core, is not unwilling;
Its claim to bondage is my poor excuse.
And giving up the ghost, that sudden spilling
Is welcome death in mutual abuse.
Perhaps submission, that a height be gained
Is just like *credo ut intelligam*,
A language game, played indoors when it rained,
Until I won it, with my finger, thumb
And one free hand, trembling with love and fear
Of what determined me, yet felt so near.

7

There's more, dear, to this kind of paradox:
We know how supple Epimetheus
With his stiff key, unlocked Pandora's box
And pushed inside, past all the fret and fuss
Toward fluttering wings of hope: she shut him up
Thereby, and fled into a world of girls,
Giggles and curiosities. His cup
Was empty, but undrained. Just so, these curls
Around your keyhole, tiny, soft and flat
Whisper together as I stroke them now,
Plot my imprisonment—once I'm in, that's that:
I'm jailed and jilted, and your binding vow
Of liberty is snapped, here on this bed.
We screw because there's nothing to be said.

8

All right! We talk too much! There are degrees
Of intimacy beyond adoration:
When Diotima took on Socrates
Their lips and tongues were chained to conversation.
A clever father of a girl once told her:
'Say something interesting, and then they'll stop.'
She soon grew wise before she was much older
And left off talking once I'd climbed on top.
But language, lighting up this darkness, shows
Far more than blackest silence can the way
Our mouths can take us. A brilliant notion goes
Down into action: we are what we say,
Knowing is feeling, telling is touching, summing
Up is attacking: being true is coming.

9

To come together, bang! on the first night
We loved would leave us little more to learn
Or hope for. But if it's you I help ignite,
When in your bed, away from you I burn.
Hope is what feeds that heat, hope that next time
Two moments of becoming flame will draw
Closer together, echoed (or in rhyme,
At least—deferring to S. de Beauvoir's law
That your explosion's too unique to mean
What mine does). It's a peculiar kind of race
When coming in first adds up to a clean
Loss; so I'll let you have a moment's grace
Now, with my hand, before the final run
Whose bang's prefigured in the starting gun.

There you are, free of mediating dress
At last, standing half-turned away from me;
For the first time my gaze's long caress
Alights on form, molds your entirety.
We'll turn again to warm, envisioning touch
Who felt through the cloth, darkly, to begin:
My eyes' light stroking can't delay too much
The finger's face-to-face of final skin.
Your image now, though, undraped and intact:
Full moon, clear of her velvet déshabille?
The destitute, cold nakedness of Fact?
Truth in her unencumbered nudity?
Venus and Truth in the old handbooks show
The same bare image you have let me know.

II

Now you walk toward me and the windowed moon,
Shedding the draperies that shadow lays
Over your pale entirety, which soon
Falls into parts, under the hands of praise.
Even the poor, trapped Paris could award
That bright, permitted fruit to none but you,
Had you been there, a fourth; but here, adored,
Your vying goddesses crowd round and sue—
Wise mouth, high-regnant breasts and lovely cunt—
For all that Discord gave me: shall I start
By honoring the Highest? Shall I hunt
Middle-ground? Is the Last the golden part?
Who waits to win, with a faint, blushing itch?
Just let me touch them, and I'll tell you which.

Remembered nights, and a few afternoons
Are all of you that I'll have left to keep
Someday, like scraps of half-forgotten tunes,
Making a feverish disease of sleep.
One morning you bent down to touch your toes:
A band of body peeped out of your jeans.
That strip of you expands, and overflows
Its bit of vision, filling other scenes:
Once after lunch we took to bed; our faces
Blurred as we still lay there in the dying light.
A taxi dropped us off at different places;
The smell of you was on my hand all night:
Each time I drained my glass, a part of you
Emptied my memory, and no one knew.

A picture of you in the golden age
Of seven in a summer by the sea
Shines from the midnight of this album-page
We hold together on your parted knee,
With braids and swayback stance and cheap sarcasm,
Newly learned, and a great solemnity
Just once, in profile. I, a pale phantasm,
Underexposed, lurk in futurity;
But in the adjacent bathhouse, through a hole
Bored in the wall, my surrogate observes,
With no great joy, your tiny crack, the sole
Treasure your body's guardianship serves:
Scratched knees, taut belly and audacious bum,
Your tiny keyhole guards the gate to come.

A sweet girl who was much too tight a fit
Taught me that being patient can be death
On making love. She just took hold of it,
Finally; we lay there, until rapid breath
Subsided. There was no point any more
To being there, bare to the autumn chill
While the pale sun crept back across the floor
And left us clinging to a distant hill
Atop the darkened bed, rather than in it.
There was no need for patience then; we stared
Up at the ceiling for what seemed a minute
Till the night came, and we were unprepared
For the soft lights outside, tears unafraid
To fall, and hopes that always fail to fade.

Upright in you, both of us vertical
As well, standing, we give but what we get;
My image in your niche, our shadows fill
The wall with our subhuman silhouette.
Some peering halfwit boy might see, and cry
'Wolf!' at this rearing animal ballet
(This dance is too precarious to try:
Better to save it for a rainy day.)
Let us then level with ourselves, and lie
Transverse, our minds no higher than our hearts,
Our pounding hearts no closer to the sky
Than all our interpenetrating parts
Some other time we'll make that godlike creature,
Crowned with its heads, joined by its baser nature.

This old, carved bed where we lie garlanded
Mirrors our intertwinings; festoons smile,
Aping the forms that Grinling Gibbons hid
In wooden mockeries of green. Meanwhile,
Crowded with ghosts, its moonlit sheets lie whitely;
We twist among them and my hands evade
Remembered openings and caves politely,
Then plunging, thankfully, into your shade.
The bed's not haunted: we have brought these spooks—
Protean partners, changing at each touch—
Locked in the moist leaves of your private books,
On the stiff finger that I use to turn them.
Blame not this grand old bed for ghosts and such,
But our poor parts of wisdom that discern them.

But as we move, surrounded by an orgy
Of all our emanations, there are others
Standing about, whose grimmer dramaturgy—
Girls and their fathers, all those boys and mothers—
Menaces from a distance, far more tragic
Than a satyric sprawl amongst ourselves
And parts of old loves, mixed by harmless magic.
From photographs, from niches and from shelves
Meanwhile, commanding silently and waiting
For the poor interlude to end, their fact
Feigns the true play, for which our penetrating
Farce can only serve as an *entr'acte:*
In an unsmiling ring around us dance
The choruses of family romance.

18

Why drink, why touch you now? If it will be
Gin from the beginning, ending there,
For me, in the unblaming rain we see
Outside your window, filling all the air?
If, in the marvellous middle of it all,
Gin-drops of sweat come splashing down like rain
On both our bodies? If, once each, we call
The other's name as if in final pain?
Why then go through with it, when to imagine
What we shall do, what we shall be, is still
The noblest work of all, the sovereign region
Enduring, green, beyond both wish and will?
Why, naked and trembling, act out such old laws?
Because because because because because.

[1962–1972]

NEW YORK

Quid Romae faciam . . .
—Juvenal, Sat. III

'Sing of New York, the—what?' exclaimed the Muse,
'My dear, you're kidding!' and turned to refuse
My true, caressing hand between her thighs
(An Argo sailing toward his golden prize).
She wiggled some, and pouted ever so,
And then those thighs swung shut against the foe.
Her legs lay parallel along the sheet
Like lines in couplets that can never meet,
Being but intersected by their rhyme
As if to say: 'No poem for you this time,
No founts, no depths of form from me tonight,
No sea-shapes and no rhythms wrung from light.
Go back to all that cultivated patter
Of rhymed iambics, and to subject matter.
"New York"—that's folly that I can't endure.
No poem: you'll have to give them literature.
And I've got better things to do.' She rose,
Dressed, cursed a zipper that refused to close,
Checked the hem of her interstellar dress
And ran off, to those better things, I guess.

Farewell! My dear old friend is leaving town
At last; and if I say this with a frown
Not of expected loss, but of chagrin
(He's running out, just as I'm moving in),
It's not because I don't admire the way

51

His urban night awakes to purer day:
Despite the bleakness of most rural sights,
Choose Adirondack over Brooklyn Heights,
Better in solitude than fear to dwell,
To yawn in heaven, than explode in hell:
Bombed houses falling on your head, crossed wires,
Rich young folks piously igniting fires,
Poisonous traffic, air awash with crud,
And august poets bawling out for blood.

His groaning U-Haul halted at the spot—
In view of Hell-Gate's vaulted arch—where not
One car a minute really can survive
From ninety-sixth street to the east side drive,
My old friend Rus got out, sat on the hood
Of his Detroit Disgusting; near him stood,
Sooty and pale, bland-visaged as a dumb thing,
A ghastly hospital—or school—or something;
A clogged, unmoving stream of traffic hid
The sluggish, filthy river as it slid
Between the welfare islands on both banks;
Smokestacks gazed down at air-enhancing tanks.
Surveying his belongings crammed within
His orange trailer—an old mandolin;
Ten yards of tweeds he'd once brought home from Nassau;
His crated Greek pot; and his Ibram Lassaw
(And what, crammed in between his carpet slippers,
  One would guess was a pair of coupon-clippers)
Part of his wardrobe; lamps; an indiscreet
Case of real '49 Chateau Lafite
He'd never broken out for me; the pearls
Of a small shell collection; his ex-girl's

Pre-amplifier and my *Lohengrin*
Leered through lacunae in the tarpaulin.

He sighed and shrugged: 'There's no more room for me.
I'm broke, and, like the air, whatever's free
Is probably poisonous: I'm off to green
Lawns wider than a color TV screen.
I've had it all; let those remain who need
The grinding crowds and the great mills of greed:
The thieving steel of the Triborough Bridge
Authority spans Pelham and Bay Ridge,
Whose Moses may have slain an overseer
Once long ago—but see his late career,
Cornering the straw market, and his boast,
Outliving Pharaohs, a rich palace ghost.
Let grasping landlords stay to plead and whimper,
And builders, whose new walls each day grow limper.
Let him who must, remain: the poorest wretch,
Chained by his indigence to a bleak stretch
Of asphalt turf; the richest, too, must stay,
Chained just to his ability to pay.

'What's in New York for me? A clever liar
I'm not, whether for purchase or for hire.
The quarrelsome and unconvivial cup
Of parties bores me, and I am fed up
With agitprop. I'm unemployable
At praising cheesey books because they're *full
Of where it's at right now*! The theatre's shit:
Broadway twaddle is only aimed to twit
The pudding sensibilities of dumb
Women, unliberated yet, who come

From out of town (or in: it doesn't make
The slightest bit of difference) and take
The seats, and as demeaning audience, the cake.
—Or go off-off-off Broadway, way down east:
You'll find it isn't better in the least.
There, "theatre must engage its viewers" and
Break down the evil boundaries that stand
Between the shower and the being shown;
Playgoers now cannot be left alone,
And so unlovely boys and solemn drabs
Mix with the audience, and give them crabs,
While "interpenetration" is so literal
It must involve the phallic and the clitoral.
Critics? They don't need me. Somewhere they'll find
Some venomous tongue, led by a minor mind
To drop, while snarling like an animal,
Yugo-Hungarian poison on it all.

'It's all too much. The old Metropolis
Was never planned to be the Bower of Bliss.
But crowding, cosmopolitan manure,
Meant that some civilization was secure:
Enough intelligent people, living in
Enough proximity, so that the din
Of louder-than-ordinary life around
Confused and comforted one with the sound.
The idiot driver's leaned-on, angry horn,
Failing to goad the beast on which he's borne,
The smashing of non-operative telephone,
Squealing of brakes, totalitarian drone
Of sirens rushing to elicit ire
With rude contempt, or to put out a fire—

Noises of busyness make their retreats
As yowling chaos reassumes the streets.'

He ceased as, through the halted traffic's mass,
A nodding youth of fourteen dragged his ass
Past a stalled ambulance, then, beyond pain,
Vanished near where a gutter may have lain.
'Diethyl morphine, tragic heroine!'
My friend continued, 'you whose only sin
Was to submit to Harrison's foul sway!
Golden and sanguine laws which tempt and slay
Forbidding, make desired and most dear
In price, what otherwise we might not fear.
Pork-barrel legislation for the mob
Keeps many a bribed narc in his nasty job.
Her sad and not unwitting victims dot
The streets, while moralists inspect their lot,
Weep, and conclude that in this happy isle
All prospects please, and only junk is vile.

'Ill fares the land that merits little praise,
Where men accumulate, and wealth decays;
Where Mulciber & Sons, Incorporated,
Builders of pre-fab ruins, unabated
Spawn their impermanent boxes everywhere,
Pasting their cheapness on the dusty air.
Imperial Rome was splendid, if confused,
But useful buildings really could be used.
Now bricklayers, plying their ancient art,
Muck up their mortar from the very start,
Take coffee breaks all day, and with a chuckle
Watch as the walls they build begin to buckle.'

He paused to watch a tired patrolman shove
One of the public he was servant of,
Who bellowed back at his blue-coated brother;
Each tried for greater rudeness than the other.
Back to his car-hood and his theme Rus leapt:
'Service, each month more grudging and inept,
Has sovietized: the languages I speak
Are only English, German, French, some Greek,
Italian, Yiddish and a bit of Gullah—
I never needed them to get a cruller
And coffee, or to give a street address:
I'm not so good at Spanish, I confess,
And so in cabs I circle through the dark
When all I wished was to traverse the park.
I'm threatened when the tip's not twice the fare.
But then, I wasn't going anywhere,
Really, just to the movies, to await
For forty minutes, freezing at the gate,
Three hours'—not dollars'—worth of naked snatch,
Amplified panting and a pilfered batch
Of glossy travel shots, with twanging sounds,
Like pharmaceuticals, making the rounds
Among an audience whose tepid praise
Is touched by memories of milder days
When Wittgenstein, and I, flicked out each night
At something mindless, beautiful and bright.'

Well, how about the Mets? They have come far . . .
'—The Mets? The Museum and the Opera?
Then, no, until the angels start to sing
At the departure of Director Bing
When there will vanish, with a mighty roar,

His audience, productions and decor.
Across the park, the other Met is ill:
You can find pots and pictures in it still
I guess, among the crowds who are lured in
Not by the touching, bronze-age safety pin,
The Dirck Bouts, or the Hellenistic head,
Beauties and truths of the unending dead,
But by the price-tag on the latest purchase.
While guards now eye us warily, and search us
For razors, car antennae, pots of grease
With which mobs humanize a masterpiece,
The Mammon of attendance figures stands
Rubbing his failing directorial hands.
Dear Hoving! let him repossess with love
Those parks he was a good commissioner of!

'Richmond and Queens? all that's a world apart
That neither touches, nor yet breaks my heart.
While evil flourishes in Washington
My loud, minority New York's the one
I'm leaving—where disgusting Mitchell breeds
Allies like flies whose hopeless, violent deeds
Augment his power; so I'm off to where
Queens is diluted in a lot of air.
Truth is in hiding, language so decayed
That I can't say I call a spade a spade
Without a chorus of *"You see, you see!*
Languageists are the real enemy!"

'Manhattan's all there is, and that's no good—
There's no equivalent of St. John's Wood.
I don't belong to the quasurban faction:

One passive sufferer in the realm of action,
Sebastian, seems to flourish in St. George,
S.I., where once the smithy's sounding forge
Rang out above the bay—a gurgling tunnel
May soon convert his village to a funnel.
We're had by that great powerfail, con Ed:
Bell's ads are lively, but their phones are dead.
Call "Operator" and you can expect
A surly girl, and with a speech defect.
Alf moved here from his house on Beacon Hill
And nightly hears, despite his sleeping-pill,
Through his thin walls on Second Avenue
His neighbors quarrel, and his neighbors screw.
His friend Ralph lives on the West Side, meanwhile,
In a well-built, half-century-old pile:
High ceilings, wide rooms out of rooms unfolding,
Where squads of roaches drill along the molding.
Ted has been mugged and Chloe has been raped;
Charles had his left ear messily reshaped;
Twelve burglaries have left poor Colin vexed—
I shall not wait around to be the next.'

Scarce had he reached the end of his complaint,
The foul air making even sunset faint,
When the loud horn, incessant and unkind,
From a pink Ford Omphalos just behind
Urged him behind his wheel; waving goodnight,
Rus vanished in the fading urban light.

My eyes strained after him, a ruby gleam
Of tail-light sinking in a sanguine stream
Stretching across the bridges, reaching out

For green, receding hills which, in the rout
Of growing dust and sinking darkness, fade
Further into the distance each decade.
I turned back toward the city then, to muse
On his bright future, with those shining views
And costly beauties of which we're in want:
Dilapidated walls in cold Vermont;
Impoverished rustics, down the road a piece,
Whose nephew was caught buggering their niece;
White cotton-batting bread for sale at all
(Both) local supermarkets. O, the ball
The firemen (volunteer) contrive each spring!
(You'll know the season's surely—er—in swing.)
Two cars; four snow tires; fifty sets of keys;
Expiring herds of handymen to please;
Forty-mile drives to fan the dying coals
Of conversation with some other souls
Who still remember what discourse can be
Among the few who don't need every 't'
Crossed in bold-face, nor a shared, dubious joint
Gasped at, in order just to grasp the point.

But let me not sip from an empty cup:
Despite such easy, juvenile bitching-up,
Trees are at best drab objects when they take
The place of people (unless you can make,
Like George the Third in his insanity,
Intelligent conversation with a tree).
Mountains are not to climb, but to remember;
Sunset on bare, wide beaches in September,
The chill of brilliant, dark Sierra nights,
Midocean loomings of the Northern Lights,

The closed, familial huddle of small towns
In winter whites, autumnal reds and browns—
All blossoming fictions, plucked just for the day,
Brought home against the truth of urban grey,
Will flower in the garden of the mind,
Their pale originals quite left behind.
But if one's sentenced to a daily view,
Nature will fail him in a day or two.
I who had undergone a banishment
(Fifteen years long in the wrong cities pent)
Replacing my fled counterpart, can sink
Into New York's congestion, fear and stink,
Untilled concrete beneath a dirty dome:
The difference is that I am moving home.
Throughout this country, one's home town contracts
After one leaves it, and remembered facts
Are paler, teachers shorter, neighborhoods
Narrowed and sunken, the beloved woods
One picnicked in a patch of scrubby alder;
Bright shops get dingy, public grass grows balder.
The older shapes of living shrink, and those
Who move among them still like ghosts, enclose
A seeming want of substance: who returns
Home again in America, but burns
With mixed embarrassment and cindered love
For everything he was the upshot of?
New York gets worse, but so does everything.
It hasn't shrunk a bit. What I could bring
Back to the city after fifteen years
Of exile hasn't melted into tears
That, partly condescending, partly fond,
Watered the ground that I had grown beyond.

I surely came back in a rush of luck:
No horrors happened in the mover's truck;
I moved all but a few things which I stored
To an apartment I can still afford
(I am part owner of the flat I rent me).
Ed Koch, my congressman, can represent me
Because there is about as much good sense
Concentrated in his constituents
As there is anywhere; my children go
To un-selfconscious school at home, and so
They feel at home in school—good luck, it's true.
But whether in China or, indeed, Peru,
In small towns, the well-favored and the wretch,
Haven't much room in which their luck can stretch.

In smaller cities, nothing much can be
Private, and all one finds is secrecy.
A crowd is not a mob, nor makes one die
A death of self inside it, with a sigh.
Only in anonymity and crowds
Can urban wanderers unwind their shrouds,
Unchained by nature in their final quest
Where largest, deepest cities are the best.
Green foliage and a backwoods road or two
Hide Appalachian poverty from view:
In the Metropolis, the hopeless poor
Decently plain, are by no means obscure.
High towers with dingy walkups at their backs
Are found disposed on both sides of the tracks;
And even urban rustics, those who live
Not in the city, but in primitive

Villages scattered in among its blight
Are led out, no great distance, into light.

Now as for homecomings—*mirabile factu!*—
New York's the only city to come back to;
Reaching Manhattan, high over the tossed
Water at Spuyten Duyvil which I crossed
Once in a kayak when I was nineteen;
Turbulent thoughts impressed upon its screen
Of surface, glittering with overlaid
Transparencies of memory, filtering shade
And repetitions animate a view
That I am more than just returning to.

Thus I live here again. My brother Mike
Has moved next door; and in a way, I'm like
Some old agrarian conservative:
The half-mile distance between where I live
And where I did when I was ten, feels never
Once like a shackle I should want to sever
Now, but like an extension of my own,
A tap-root run through asphalt, pipe and stone—
Plenty of continuity for an
Otherwise rootless cosmopolitan.
But memory has its hearsay too: my great-
Grandfather came in 1848,
Fleeing from fuzz and new defenestrations
In Prague, to wander here among the nations,
Bring up his dozen children, make cigars,
And live for me in anecdote, like stars,
Those tiny innuendoes, piercing night,
From which a child infers a plain of light.

My grandfather and I walked in the park
Around the frozen lake, in growing dark;
In 1888, he said, the year
Of the great blizzard, we crossed without fear.
I listened as the bundled skaters skimmed
The gray ice on the safe part that was rimmed
With benches, cut across the reflex of
A starry park lamp on the bridge above.
Who was remembering, and who had merely
Heard of the past? For each it gleamed as clearly.

Now nested memories open up again:
My older daughter, at the age of ten,
Hears of the old Met Opera House from me,
Some half-formed fiction she will never see,
As at the same age, I was quite at home
With a remembrance called the Hippodrome—
Phased, similar emblems of the city's quest,
Moving beyond historic palimpsest,
For instant self-fulfillment. One night late,
Six years ago in August, through the great
Newly revealed vaults in a ruined, weird
Penn Station, winds sang and faint stars appeared
Above columnar bases; broken gloom
Swallowed the crystal-palace waiting room
In gaping Piranesian pits—all seemed
Somehow created for this, and redeemed
By that great wind-swept moment. Then I passed
Out onto the hot pavements, to be gassed
By buses, bumped by derelicts, away
From dreams of change to contact with decay.—

But so much more decay because we've got
Riches to moulder, and so much to rot.

Tim lives downtown, and makes a long commute
(To Queens, to work) as long as is the route
Deep into Westchester; he gets to go
Home to a lovely place on Bank Street, though;
Not the benighted suburb, Middle Ridge
Where affluence is underprivilege.
Jim lives in Athens; there's no need to roam;
Our ruins-and-fig republic here at home
Will mellow us, as things go to the bad,
And lend us patience that we've never had.
Then, as our science fails and our arts rot,
Instead of huddling in some minor spot
On the torn outskirts of a little town
(Where more than here, old buildings are torn down,
And metal siding fronts for honest wood)
We'll see the ending out from where we should:
With nothing working, services gone slack,
Mushrooms on the abandoned subway track,
Telephones silent between twelve and two,
Thousands of cats reclaim an empty zoo.

West in Manhattan where the sun has set
The elevator rises calmly yet
In my dark tower, against the tower-dimmed sky,
Whose wide, old windows yield my narrower eye
Images no revision can defeat:
Newspapers blown along the empty street
At three A.M. (somewhere in between 'odd,'
A guru told me long ago, and 'God');

Calm steam rising from manholes in the dark;
Clean asphalt of an avenue; the spark
Of gold in every mica window high
On westward faces of the peaks; the sky
Near dawn, framed in the zig-zag canyon rim
Of cross-streets; bits of distant bridge, the dim
Lustrous ropes of pale lights dipping low;
Rivers unseen beneath, sable and slow.

Gardens? Lead me not home to them: a plain
Of rooftops, gleaming after April rain
In later sunlight, shines with Ceres' gold
Sprung up, not ripped, from earth; gained as of old.
Our losses are of gardens. We create
A dense, sad city for our final state.

[1970]

EPILOGUE
the loss of smyrna

Sick and weak I lay, as the dreadful winter
Drank my life's last wine, and the dreams of prouder
Days and loud, sweet nights seemed to snap and splinter
        Into a powder.

Sick and weak; till then I remembered SMYRNA,
Port of Venus! city of figs and quinces!
Where the poor, tired wanderer yet can earn a
        Pleasure of princes.

So I hied me off on an evil steamer,
Crewed by cast-off Lascars, and captained madly.
Mascot mastiffs fought for a human femur;
        Cabins smelt badly;

Passengers drugged down far below all sinning
Only made me hungrier for the seaside
Deeply dreamed, whose domes and delights, beginning
        Down by the quayside,

Reach away back up into hidden altars
Where the sacrifices to final pleasure
By the one, dark ardor that never falters
        Last beyond measure.

Borne thus bravely over despairing's ocean
By the wild, bright dream of those domes, and reaching

Port at last, I joyed at the end of motion,
             Firmness of beaching.

But no domes saw I! It was like Biloxi,
Mississippi! I was dismayed and nearly
Screamed 'Oi Weh! Izmir!' But a passing doxy
             (She'd gone to Brearley

Thence to Radcliffe), speaking in pear-shaped diphthongs
Said, 'Why this *is* Smyrna, dearie!' and quoting
Other poems by Auden, unlaced her hip-thongs
             Slowly emoting.

Moonlit twin domes gleamed then! And oriental
Towers rose; courts; gardens that seem to burn a
Flame within my memory still! No mental
             Yearning, but SMYRNA!

Then she led me back to an ancient quarter
Where the town's joys lay, to a house where seven
Sisters who looked each like the others' daughter
             Guarded a heaven.

Seven? Nay, more nearly a hundred ladies
Filled that Empyrean with their equipment,
Bubbling, tossed, twitched, jouncing; and half of Hades,
             Ready for shipment,

Waited down boats' holds or in lazaretted
Cellars near Seine, Thames, or the Rhine's conflation
Hard by Basel—maidens awaiting fêted
             Pleasure's purgation.

There the rainbow pales in ashamed abasement
Under such wide, variegated spectra!
Antique illustrations in every casement:
                    Reddened Electra

There goes down on a yet-arrested brother,
Bound and lashed; and Circe outdoes herself there:
Half her own sex, turned into half another,
                    Over a shelf there.

Visions! dreams! joys! promises of eternal
Freedoms! bondages far beyond describing
Catalogued on welcoming flasks of Smyrnal
                    Things for imbibing.

There the warm will stints not, and there the flesh is
Even more than eager for overreaching,
Where a white form, crossed with the crimson meshes
                    Shows the rod's teaching.

There, too, Spring and Fall are maintained together
Both at once, as in every perfect Bower:
Nine-year-olds and their grandpas play touch-feather
                    Hour by hour.

Frontal voyagings! and severe excursions
Into backward countries, where dark, unmasking
Secrets yield themselves! even furred diversions!
                    —All for the asking.

Vast, complex arrangements for feet: a fire,
Heating steel shoes (there are so many martyrs!)

And, to draw those torturing buskins higher,
        Horrible garters!

Even you, dear friend, looking down to greet me
From a balcony over someone's shoulder
(She, the meanwhile, wriggling) appeared to meet me
        Looking much bolder

Than you have ever been. As I moved, saluting,
Suddenly Night fell—not a night of blisses
Filled with Smyrning raptures—but reedy fluting,
        Turning to hisses,

Surged behind my temples and—blink and swallow—
There I lay. Cold winter had just uncrowned me.
SMYRNA? Gone! gone in a vision's hollow
        Smashing around me.

Where again shall pain be redeemed in blessings?
Where else may we see such a fierce, a stern, a
Hard and iron touch make such sweet caressings?
        Where, but in SMYRNA!

When again in dream or in sickly vision
Shall I, then, with thirteen young ladies turn a
Banquet into such a complex elision?
        Never in SMYRNA!

[1965]

Town and Country Matters *was printed in a trade edition of 3,850 and a deluxe edition of 150 at the press of David R. Godine. The design is by Carol Shloss, press work by Susan Ward. The type, Aldine Bembo, was set by A. Colish, Inc. of Mount Vernon, New York. All the books were printed on Warren's Olde Style Wove and were bound by Alan Horowitz.*